Wok

BARNES
&NOBLE
BOOKS
NEW YORK

Contents

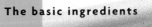

Infinite variety
The basic ingredients

Asian cuisine is varied and healthy, its basic ingredients: lots of fresh vegetables, just a little meat, lean fish and a never ending variety of deliciously aromatic spices, pastes and sauces – some hot, some less so. Traditional noodles or steamed rice are served with almost all dishes. Fragrant rice from Thailand and Japanese sticky rice are particularly popular. Noodles made from rice flour have the advantage of not needing to be cooked: simply soak them for a few minutes in warm water. As Far Eastern cuisine gains more and more devotees, many herbs, spices, vegetables and other ingredients essential in Asian wok cookery are often already available in well-stocked supermarkets. The exotic or unusual can be obtained from specialist Asian retailers. All ingredients should be as fresh as possible. The short cooking time required in wok cooking means that most vitamins are retained, making the wok a healthy alternative in the kitchen. And once you have enjoyed the fresh aromas and unbeatable flavor of cooking with fresh ginger or lemon grass, you will not be tempted again to substitute the powdered or dried kind in your cooking.

1

SCALLIONS (left), also known as spring or green onions, have a mild flavor. Their peppery green stalks are also a great favorite in wok cookery.

1 CHILIES, the fiery hot relatives of red peppers, add pungency to wok dishes. Unripe chilies are green, ripe chilies are red. In general, small chilies are stronger than large ones.

2 BAMBOO SHOOTS are the young shoots of the bamboo plant. They are harvested like asparagus: when they reach a height of 1 foot, they are cut down. Generally they are only available in cans.

3 RICE WINE is significantly milder than ordinary vinegar due to its lower acidity content of just three per cent.

4 SHIITAKE MUSHROOMS, also known as black mushrooms or Black Forest mushrooms, have a strong aroma. They are available all year round.

5 BASMATI is the most prized long-grain rice with its delicate taste and characteristic fragrance. It is also known as fragrant rice and is particularly suitable for stir-frying.

6 CILANTRO has many uses in Asian cuisine: fresh cilantro, also known as Chinese parsley, has a sharp, lemony flavor, and is used much as curly parsley is used in Western cooking. The roots taste even stronger than the leaves. Coriander seeds have a flowery, sweet aroma and a taste rather like orange peel.

7 GINGER can be spicy and fruity or burning hot, depending on how much is used. Fresh ginger has better flavor than the powder form.

7

NOODLES in Asia are typically made from wheat or buckwheat flours. Rice noodles (made from rice flour), and transparent bean thread noodles, which are made from mung bean starch, are a particular speciality.

SOY SAUCE is seen as the universal seasoning in Asian cuisine. The favorites are the dark, salty sauces from China and Japan. Light soy sauce is saltier and is used in fish and vegetable dishes, so they retain their light, bright color.

TAMARIND is revered as a flavoring, with its fruity but slightly sour taste, especially in Thai and Indonesian cooking. Here it is usually only available as tamarind pulp sold in blocks in Asian supermarkets.

TOFU is a staple food in Asia and is made from curdled soybean milk. It comes in block form and is rich in protein and low in cholesterol. It has a very mild, almost bland taste and calls for the addition of lots of spices.

LEMON GRASS is a woody plant. Only the lower tender part above the root is used. Lemon grass gives food a lemony fragrance and flavor and adds a slight sourness.

6

Step by Step
The essential cooking techniques

Amateur and professional cooks alike are unanimous about its versatility: boiling, roasting, steaming, shallow-frying, stewing, stir-frying, or deep-frying – you can do it all in a wok! This wide, bowl-shaped pan can be used to cook almost anything. Traditional woks are made from beaten iron or steel. Modern versions are made from aluminium, which allows for good, even heat distribution. The wok works best on a gas stove. To obtain better stability and heat conductivity on an electric stove, a wok with a flat bottom should be used. Most woks measure from 12 to 16 inches in diameter. Choose a larger model, since they come in handy for cooking individual portions, as well as larger quanties, and much faster, due to a larger surface area. For steaming and stewing a wok should have a lid, which is usually supplied with it. A wok scoop is also useful, as is a metal rack which can be hung over the inside edge of the wok. You will need a bamboo brush to clean an iron wok. You will most likely find everything else you need readily available in your kitchen.

How to prepare chilies

1 Wash the chilies and pat dry. Halve the pods lengthways with a kitchen knife.

2 Remove the stem, white inner membranes, and remove the seeds. Rinse the peppers and leave to drain.

3 Cut the peppers into rings. Note: they are very strong, so wear rubber gloves or wash your hands when you have finished!

How to prepare lemon gras

1 Cut away the outer leaves and the upper, dry half of the lemon grass stalks. Wash the remaining stalks and dry with paper towels.

2 Break the stalks into pieces and cut lengthways. Add the pieces during cooking, but remove them just before serving.

3 Alternatively, chop the stalks finely with a knife so that they can be readily eaten as part of the dish.

How to do it, step by step

1 Meat that is to be stir-fried in the wok must always be cut into bite-sized pieces.

2 Stir soy sauce, rice wine and spices together to make a marinade. Mix in the meat and leave to infuse for 15 minutes.

3 Meanwhile prepare all the other ingredients, such as vegetables, and measure out the spices so they are ready for use.

4 Stir-fry ingredients one by one and set aside in a warm place. Finally mix everything together, season and leave to infuse for several minutes.

Stir-frying – simple to do

1 Prepare all ingredients and have the necessary spices ready. Heat the wok until it is very hot and only then add a little oil.

2 Fry ingredients in the order of their cooking time, stirring continuously until they are just tender. Move anything cooked to the edge of the wok until everything is ready.

Simple wok dishes

1 Have all ingredients ready. Cook any ingredients, such as noodles or rice, according to the instructions on the packet.

2 Stir-fry the main ingredients one by one in the wok. Begin with the meat, if there is any, then set aside in a warm place.

3 Briefly stir-fry vegetables that have been cut into fine strips or small dice. Blanch larger pieces first before frying them in the wok.

4 After all the ingredients are cooked, reheat briefly together in the wok. Season with the spices and leave for a short while for the flavors to develop.

Vegetarian

Coleslaw
with Peanuts

A yellow, red and white salad: finely chopped cabbage and fresh, juicy red peppers combine with a honey-based dressing to make a crunchy, vitamin-rich treat

Ingredients

1 ¼ cups (5 oz) **white cabbage**

1 large **fennel bulb**

1 **red pepper**

1 **yellow pepper**

2 tablespoons **sesame oil**

2 **red chilies**

4 tablespoons **soy sauce**

4 teaspoons **honey**

salt

Szechuan pepper

4 tablespoons **roasted peanuts**

Preparation
SERVES 4

1 Prepare the white cabbage: wash and dry thoroughly in a salad spinner. Cut or shred into fine strips. Wash and dry the fennel and also shred finely. Wash, core and seed the peppers, and cut into fine strips.

2 Heat a wok and pour in the oil. Stir-fry the cabbage and fennel strips for 2 minutes without browning. Leave to cool.

3 Wash and seed the chilies, and chop very finely.

4 Make a salad dressing with the soy sauce, chopped chilies, honey, salt and a pinch of Szechuan pepper.

5 Combine the cooled cabbage and fennel strips with the salad dressing and leave in the refrigerator for 20 minutes to marinate. Scatter over the peanuts before serving

Those who like their food raw can also prepare an Asian-style salad without using the wok at all: replace the white cabbage with zucchini and the red pepper with a large red onion cut into fine strips.

Tofu Bites
with Lime Butter

Quick to prepare and refreshing on a hot summer's day:
marinated tofu is one of the highlights of Asian cuisine

Ingredients

2 limes

3 tablespoons **light soy sauce**

1 teaspoon **freshly ground
black pepper**

1 teaspoon **sugar**

1 lb fresh **tofu**

½ cup (4 oz) **butter**

4 tablespoons **vegetable oil**

Preparation
SERVES 4

1 Wash and dry the limes. Finely grate the rind of one lime. Halve
   both limes and juice them.

2 Prepare a marinade using the soy sauce, pepper, sugar and
   2 tablespoons of the lime juice, stirring until the sugar has
   completely dissolved.

3 Cut the tofu into ½-inch thick slices. Brush on both sides with the
   marinade. Let stand for 15 minutes.

4 Cream the butter until fluffy. Stir in the lime rind and the rest of
   the lime juice, a little bit at a time.

5 Heat a wok until very hot and add the oil. Fry the tofu slices on
   both sides until golden brown.

6 Spread the lime butter over the tofu slices, allowing it to melt.
   Take the tofu bites out of the wok and serve immediately on a
   warmed plate. Sprinkle with coarsely ground pepper to taste.

**If you prefer something crispier, give the
marinated tofu a crumb coating: after
marinating dip the tofu slices first in flour,
then in beaten egg and finally, in corn meal.
Fry on both sides until golden brown.**

Sweet and Sour Vegetables
with Pineapple and Ginger

Simply irresistible: sweet and sour dishes are traditional in Asian cuisine.
Colorful, crunchy vegetables tempt the discerning palate with a hint of sourness

Ingredients

1 cup (4 oz) **Chinese cabbage**

½ cup (4 oz) **carrots**

½ cup (4 oz) **shiitake mushrooms**

½ cup (4 oz) **snow peas**

1-inch piece fresh **ginger**

2 cloves of **garlic**

2 **red chilies**

½ cup (4 oz) tinned **bamboo shoots**

¾ cup (6 oz) fresh **pineapple**

4 tablespoons **sunflower oil**

4 tablespoons **rice vinegar**

4 tablespoons **soy sauce**

4 tablespoons **sherry**

2 tablespoons **sugar**

1 cup (8 fl oz) **chicken stock**

1 teaspoon **cornstarch**

Preparation
SERVES 4

1 Wash the Chinese cabbage, shake dry, halve the leaves lengthways and cut into ¾-inch strips. Peel the carrots and cut into thin slices. Wipe the mushrooms with paper towels and halve or quarter according to size. Wash the snow peas and cut in half.

2 Peel the ginger and cut into very fine slices. Peel and finely chop the garlic. Wash and seed the chilies and cut into fine strips.

3 Drain the bamboo shoots in a sieve. Peel the pineapple, remove the core and cut the flesh into chunks.

4 Heat a wok and add the oil. Stir-fry the carrots and mushrooms, then add the Chinese cabbage and snow peas and stir-fry briefly. Add the ginger, garlic and chilies and stir-fry briefly. Lastly add the bamboo shoots, pineapple, vinegar, soy sauce, sherry and sugar. Pour in ¾ cup of the stock and stir.

5 Mix the cornstarch with the rest of the cold stock, pour over the vegetables and stir in quickly. Leave to simmer for 2 minutes.

A good alternative to Chinese cabbage which is similar in appearance but has a much finer flavor is a type of Asian cabbage called bok choy. Bok choy is also known as Chinese white cabbage.

Sweet and Sour Tofu
with Vegetables

Preparation
SERVES 4

1 Cut the tofu into 1-inch cubes. Mix the soy sauce and sweet and sour sauce together and leave the tofu cubes to marinate for 30 minutes.

2 Wash and prepare the scallions, carrots and peppers, and cut into strips.

3 Peel the pineapple, remove the core and cut the flesh into chunks.

4 Heat a wok and add the oil. Stir-fry the vegetables until just tender. Add the tofu cubes and washed bean sprouts and stir-fry briefly.

5 Mix in the prepared pineapple chunks and stir-fry briefly. Combine the cornstarch with 1 cup (8 fl oz) water and then add the ketchup, soy sauce and sherry vinegar. Pour the mixture over the stir-fried vegetables and leave to simmer for a few minutes, until thickened.

Ingredients

¾ lb **tofu**

3 tablespoons **soy sauce**

4 tablespoons **sweet and sour sauce**

8 **scallions**

3 **carrots**

2 **red peppers**

1 ¼ cups (10 oz) fresh **pineapple**

2 tablespoons **sesame oil**

1 ½ cups (6 oz) **bean sprouts**

2 teaspoons **cornstarch**

3 tablespoons **ketchup**

4 tablespoons each **soy sauce** and **sherry vinegar**

Ingredients

1 lb white cabbage · 1 red pepper

1 cup (8 oz) fresh pineapple

1 stalk lemon grass · 1 green chili

2 tablespoons light soy sauce

4 tablespoons sherry

1 teaspoon chili sauce

salt · ½ teaspoon Szechuan pepper

1 teaspoon cornstarch

2 tablespoons desiccated coconut

1 tablespoon sesame seeds

½ teaspoon grated lemon peel

4 tablespoons vegetable oil

2 cups (8 oz) mung bean sprouts

Stir-fried White Cabbage
with Fresh Pineapple

Preparation
SERVES 4

1 Wash and prepare the cabbage and pepper, and cut into thin strips. Peel the pineapple, remove the core and cut the flesh into chunks. Trim, wash and chop the lemon grass. Wash and seed the chili and cut into fine strips.

2 Whisk the soy sauce, chili sauce, salt, pepper and cornstarch together in a small bowl.

3 Dry roast the coconut and sesame seeds in a wok until golden brown. Mix with the lemon rind.

4 Heat the wok and add the oil. Stir-fry the strips of cabbage and red pepper until just tender. Add the pineapple, lemon grass, chili and washed bean sprouts, then stir in the sauce mixture. Cook together for a further 2 minutes and serve sprinkled with the coconut and sesame seed mixture.

Dim Sum
with Onions and Bean Sprouts

Typically Asian: these little snacks with their spicy fillings

are quick to make and always good for a surprise treat

Ingredients

2 scallions

½ yellow pepper

1 red chili

1 clove garlic

½ cup (2 oz) bean sprouts

2 tablespoons sesame oil

⅓ cup soy sauce

½ lb round wonton wrappers
(about 16)

1 egg white

1 tablespoon stem ginger
in syrup

Preparation
SERVES 4

1 Trim and wash the scallions and yellow pepper and cut into small dice. Wash the chili, remove the seeds and chop very finely. Peel the garlic and also chop finely. Rinse the bean sprouts in cold water in a sieve, drain and chop roughly.

2 Heat the oil in a wok. Cook the bean sprouts, scallions, diced pepper, chili and garlic in the wok for 2 minutes. Season with 1 tablespoon of the soy sauce and leave to cool.

3 Place 1 teaspoon filling on center of 1 wonton wrapper. Fold wonton wrapper over filling, sealing the edge with a little egg white.

4 Steam for 10 minutes in the wok in either a bamboo basket or other steamer. Mix the stem ginger and the rest of the soy sauce together and serve as a dipping sauce.

An alternative tasty accompaniment is a piquant herb dressing made from 1 tablespoon freshly chopped cilantro leaves, 2 tablespoons sesame oil, 3 tablespoons soy sauce, 2 tablespoons lime juice, 1 teaspoon finely chopped garlic and a little sambal ulek.

Vegetable Balls
with Yogurt

Preparation

SERVES 4

1 Prepare and wash the vegetables. Grate the carrot and celery root coarsely, dice the red pepper, cut the cabbage leaves into thin strips, and the scallions into thin rings.

2 Put the vegetables into a bowl, add the washed bean sprouts, soy sauce, herbs and spices and mix together well. Gradually stir in the eggs and flour alternately.

3 Leave the dough to rest for 30 minutes, and test to see if it can be moulded into shapes. If necessary, add more flour.

4 Shape the dough into equal-sized balls. Heat the oil in a wok until it is very hot and deep-fry the balls individually. Lift out with a slotted spoon and leave to drain on paper towels. Serve with the yogurt.

Ingredients

1 large **carrot** · 1 cup (4 oz) **Savoy cabbage**

1 cup (4 oz) **celery root** · ½ **red pepper**

4 **scallions**

½ cup (4 oz) **mung bean sprouts**

2 tablespoons **soy sauce**

1 chopped **garlic clove**

1 tablespoon chopped **cilantro leaves**

1 ½ teaspoons grated **ginger**

1 teaspoon **curry powder**

freshly ground **black pepper** · **salt**

3 **eggs** · 6–7 tablespoons **flour**

oil for deep frying

⅔ cup (5 fl oz) natural **yogurt**

Ingredients

1 ½ cups (7 oz) **whole wheat flour**

1 **egg** · 1 **egg yolk**

2 pinches **salt**

1 tablespoon finely chopped **basil**

½ lb **cherry tomatoes**

¾ lb **button mushrooms**

2 **leeks**

oil for deep-frying

1 **lime**

Vegetable Fritters
with Lime Juice

Preparation
SERVES 4

1 Make a smooth batter with half the flour, the egg, egg yolk, 1 cup (8 fl oz) of water, salt and basil. Let stand for 15 minutes.

2 Wash the cherry tomatoes and pat dry. Wipe the mushrooms with paper towels. Trim and wash the leeks, and slice them diagonally into pieces about ¾-inch long.

3 Heat the oil in a wok until it is very hot.

4 First roll the vegetables in the rest of the flour, then dip them into the batter using a fork. Place the pieces immediately in the hot fat and fry until golden brown.

5 Drain the vegetable fritters on paper towels. Wash the lime, pat dry and cut into wedges.

6 Serve the vegetable fritters with the lime wedges.

Spring Rolls
Filled with Vegetables

The classic vegetarian dish - bean sprouts, Chinese mushrooms
and carrots make a deliciously crunchy filling

Ingredients

1 ⅔ cups (8 oz) **bread flour**

1 teaspoon **salt**

2 large **carrots**

2 cups (8 oz) **bok choy**

4 **scallions**

1 cup (5 oz) **shiitake mushrooms**

3 tablespoons each **sesame oil**
and **rice wine**

4 tablespoons **soy sauce**

2 cups (8 oz) **bean sprouts**

freshly ground **black pepper**

chili powder

1 tablespoon grated **ginger**

1 tablespoon chopped
cilantro leaves

2 tablespoons **roasted sesame
seeds**

1 **egg white** · **oil** for deep-frying

Preparation
SERVES 4

1 Add ⅔ cup (5 fl oz) lukewarm water to the flour and salt and knead together to form an elastic dough. Wrap in a damp cloth and leave to stand for 2 hours. On a floured board roll out the dough until it is paper thin and cut into 8 equal-sized rectangles.

2 Wash the vegetables. Peel the carrots. Cut the carrots and bok choy into very fine strips. Wash the scallions and cut into thin slices. Clean the mushrooms and slice thinly.

3 Heat a wok and add the oil. Stir-fry the vegetables for 5 minutes, then pour in the rice wine and soy sauce and allow to thicken. Stir in the bean sprouts. Season with pepper and chili powder to taste. Stir in the ginger, cilantro and sesame seeds.

4 Leave the filling to cool briefly, then put a spoonful onto each rectangle of pastry. Fold in both long sides of the rectangle and then roll up from the narrow end. Brush the edges with a little egg white and press firmly together.

5 Clean the wok, the add the oil and heat until very hot. Deep-fry the spring rolls one by one for about 5 minutes until golden brown, turning over once.

Spinach and feta cheese make a very tasty filling: mix together 1 lb blanched, chopped spinach, 6 chopped scallions, 2 crushed garlic cloves and ½ lb cubed feta cheese.

Spinach
with Tofu and Sesame Seeds

Preparation
SERVES 4

1 Trim the spinach and rinse briefly in cold water. Bring a good half inch of water to the boil in a wok, add the salt and then the spinach. Cover with a lid and cook until the spinach has wilted, then rinse with cold water and leave to drain in a colander. Roughly chop the spinach and divide between four soup bowls.

2 Cut the tofu into small cubes (about ½-inch square). Peel the garlic and slice thinly.

3 Toast the sesame seeds in the wok over medium-low heat. Remove and set to one side. Heat half of the oil in the wok and roast the garlic until golden brown. Mix the soy sauce with the rest of the oil, the sugar and the rice wine, pour over the garlic and heat. Stir in the roasted sesame seeds.

4 Add the tofu cubes and heat through. Spoon over the spinach and serve warm.

Ingredients

½ lb **spinach**

1 teaspoon **salt**

⅓ lb **tofu**

2 cloves **garlic**

2 tablespoons **sesame seeds**

2 tablespoons **sesame oil**

1 tablespoon **soy sauce**

1 tablespoon **sugar**

1 tablespoon **rice wine**

Ingredients

1 small **cauliflower**

6 **carrots** · 4 baby **zucchini**

4 **scallions** · 1 red **chili**

salt · 3 tablespoons **butter**

pinch **saffron threads**

1 teaspoon **turmeric**

½ teaspoon ground **ginger**

½ teaspoon **cumin**

freshly ground **black pepper**

3 tablespoons **lemon juice**

14-oz can unsweetened **coconut milk**

2 tablespoons chopped **cilantro leaves**

Mixed Rainbow Vegetables
with Turmeric and Saffron

Preparation
SERVES 4

1 Wash and prepare the vegetables. Separate the cauliflower into florets. Halve the carrots and quarter the zucchini lengthways, then cut both into 1-inch long pieces. Chop the scallions into large pieces. Seed the chili and cut into fine strips.

2 Bring half an inch of water to the boil in a wok and add the salt. Cook the cauliflower florets for 4 minutes with the lid on. Add the carrots and cook together

for 3 minutes longer. Pour off the water and leave the vegetables to drain. Melt the butter in the wok. Stir-fry the chili, saffron, turmeric, ginger and cumin.

3 Add the cauliflower, carrots, zucchini and scallions, mix together and stir-fry for 4 minutes.

4 Season with salt and pepper, stir in the lemon juice and coconut milk, bring to the boil and stir in the cilantro.

Scrambled Eggs
with Chinese Mushrooms

Inexpensive but very impressive: simple scrambled eggs
are cleverly transformed in a jiffy into an exotic spicy snack

Ingredients

3 dried **morel mushrooms**

3 dried **shiitake mushrooms**

1 small **red chili**

¼-inch piece fresh **ginger**

2 **scallions**

2 sprigs **cilantro**

4 **eggs**

2 teaspoons **soy sauce**

freshly ground **black pepper**

1 teaspoon **peanut oil**

1 teaspoon **corn oil**

Preparation
SERVES 4

1 Put the dried mushrooms in a bowl and add enough hot water to cover. Leave to soak for 15 minutes.

2 Wash the chilies, remove the seeds and cut into fine strips. Peel the ginger and chop very finely. Trim the scallions, wash and cut into fine strips. Wash the cilantro, shake dry and remove the leaves.

3 Drain the mushrooms and cut into pieces. Beat the eggs and stir in the soy sauce, pepper to taste, and the peanut oil.

4 Heat a wok and add the oil. Stir-fry the mushrooms briefly. Then add the rest of the ingredients, except for the eggs, and mix with the mushrooms. Pour in the beaten eggs and cook until they begin to set, pushing the mixture to the edge of the wok as it solidifies.

5 Serve the scrambled eggs on warmed plates or in small bowls, garnished with the cilantro.

This scrambled egg dish can, of course, also be made with fresh mushrooms. Only wash the mushrooms if they are especially dirty. Otherwise it is sufficient just to wipe them with dry paper towels.

Noodles & Rice

Bean Thread Noodles
with Shrimp and Mushrooms

A treat for all fans of the Orient - bean thread noodles with shrimp is a hot favorite
that is available on almost every street corner in China

Ingredients

¾ lb peeled **shrimp**

2 oz dried **morel mushrooms**

4 cloves **garlic**

1 dried **chili**

½ lb **snow peas**

½ lb small **mushrooms**

1 can **baby corncobs**

¼ lb fresh **tofu**

1 tablespoon grated fresh **ginger**

4 tablespoons **sesame oil**

3 tablespoons **soy sauce**

2 tablespoons **oyster sauce**

salt

pepper

¾ lb **bean thread noodles**

Preparation
SERVES 4

1 Rinse the shrimp in cold water in a sieve and leave to drain. Pour
hot water over the dried mushrooms and leave to soak for
15 minutes. Then drain and wash them well so that any remaining
sand is removed.

2 Peel the garlic cloves and cut in half. Pound the chili very finely
with a pestle and mortar. Trim and wash the snow peas. Wipe the
mushrooms with a damp paper towel and cut evenly into slices.
Drain the baby corncobs and cut into quarters lengthways. Cut the
tofu into cubes. Peel the ginger and grate finely.

3 Heat up a wok and add the oil. Over a high heat stir-fry first the
snow peas, then the mushrooms, garlic and dried mushrooms one
after the other for about 2 minutes after each addition. Push the
vegetables to the edge of the wok and add the baby corncobs,
shrimp and cubed tofu. Fry everything for about 1 minute over
high heat, stirring occasionally.

4 Add the soy sauce, grated ginger, oyster sauce and pounded chili.
Mix the vegetables well with the shrimp and the spices, season to
taste with salt and pepper and fry for about 1 minute.

5 Immerse the bean thread noodles in boiling water and leave to
soak for about 10 minutes. Strain, rinse with warm water, and leave
to drain for a short while. Mix with the shrimp and vegetables
and serve hot.

Exotic Stir-fried Rice
with Apples and Fish

A rice creation with a Far Eastern touch: shrimp and fish meet apples,
raisins and beansprouts for a culinary rendez-vous

Ingredients

1 large **onion**

¾ lb **fennel**

1 **red pepper**

1 ½ cups **beansprouts**

3 tablespoons **sesame oil**

1 cup **rice**

2 tablespoons **soy sauce**

1 lb **ocean perch fillets**

1 tablespoon **lemon juice**

½ lb **apples**

¼ lb peeled **shrimp**

⅓ cup **raisins**

1 teaspoon dried **dill**

Preparation
SERVES 4

1 Peel the onion and cut into small dice. Wash and prepare the
fennel and pepper and cut into thin strips. Wash the beansprouts
and leave to drain.

2 Heat up a wok and add the oil. Cook the diced onion until
transparent, add the rice and stir-fry briefly. Add the strips of
fennel and pepper and stir-fry it all together for about 10 minutes.
Pour in 1 cup water and the soy sauce and leave to simmer for
25 minutes.

3 Cut the fish into 3-inch pieces, sprinkle with the lemon juice and
leave to marinate for 10 minutes. Meanwhile peel and core the
apples, cut into quarters, and slice thinly.

4 Put the slices of apple and the pieces of fish in the wok and leave
to marinate for 10 minutes. Rinse the shrimp in cold water in a
sieve, leave to drain for a short while and then add to the fish and
rice.

5 Carefully stir in the raisins, beansprouts and dill. Let all the
flavors combine together for a further 2 minutes and serve
garnished with fresh dill to taste.

**The apples with the best aroma for this
stir-fried rice recipe are a slightly sour
variety which will not soften too quickly
during cooking, such as Granny Smith.**

Chinese Egg Noodles
with Chicken and Shrimp

Preparation
SERVES 4

1 Bring plenty of salted water to boil in a large saucepan. Add the Chinese noodles and bring back to the boil, separating the noodles with chopsticks, and leave to soften for 2 to 3 minutes. Strain in a colander, rinse with cold water and leave to drain thoroughly.

2 Trim and wash the scallions, and cut into slices. Peel and chop the garlic. Cut the chicken breast fillet into strips. Wash and seed the chili, and chop finely.

3 Heat up a wok and add the oil. Stir-fry the prepared ingredients in the wok: First put in the meat and stir-fry. Then add the shrimp and fry with the meat. Finally add the garlic and scallions, followed by the chopped chili.

4 Before serving add the washed beansprouts, spices and noodles to the wok and toss everything lightly together.

Ingredients

salt

¾ lb **Chinese egg noodles**

1 bunch **scallions**

2 cloves **garlic**

¾ lb boneless, skinless **chicken breast**

1 **chili**

4 tablespoons **vegetable oil**

¼ lb peeled **shrimp**

½ cup **beansprouts**

1 tablespoon grated fresh **ginger**

4 tablespoons **soy sauce**

Ingredients

¾ lb **Chinese egg noodles**

salt

1 small head **Chinese cabbage**

¼ lb **shiitake mushrooms**

¾ lb **pork tenderloin**

1 **red chili**

3 tablespoons **vegetable oil**

1 tablespoon grated fresh **ginger**

1 stalk **lemongrass**

½ tsp **Chinese five spice powder**

2 tablespoons **rice wine**

4 tablespoons **soy sauce**

Indonesian-style Noodles
with Pork

Preparation
SERVES 4

1 Place the noodles in boiling salted water, bring back to the boil, separate with chopsticks, and leave to soak for 2 to 3 minutes. Then strain in a colander, rinse in cold water and leave to drain thoroughly.

2 Wash and prepare the Chinese cabbage, and cut into ½-inch wide strips. Wipe the mushrooms with a damp paper towel. Thinly slice the mushrooms and meat.

3 Wash the chili, cut in half lengthways, remove the seeds and chop finely.

4 Heat up a wok and add the oil. Stir-fry the meat, mushrooms and cabbage one after the other. Add the spices and pour over the rice wine and soy sauce. Stir in the noodles and leave to stand for 3 minutes.

Rice Noodles
with Thai Basil

The aromatic fragrance gives this dish its uniquely subtle character:

Thai basil and rice noodles offer the palate a perfectly balanced combination

Ingredients

½ lb wide **rice noodles**

4 cloves **garlic**

4 **shallots**

2 each **red** and **green chilies**

2 sprigs Thai or ordinary **basil**

½ lb **beef tenderloin**

4 tablespoons **vegetable oil**

salt

2 tablespoons **oyster sauce**

2 tablespoons **fish sauce**

1 tablespoon **sugar**

1 tablespoon **vinegar**

1 teaspoon powdered **beef stock**

Preparation
SERVES 4

1 Leave the rice noodles to soak for 10 minutes in warm water. Drain, and using scissors cut the noodles into 4-inch lengths.

2 Peel the garlic cloves and shallots, wash and seed the chilies. Crush together with a pestle and mortar, or purée in a food processor.

3 Wash the basil and pat dry. Pluck off the leaves and chop roughly. Cut the beef into thin strips.

4 Heat up a wok and add the oil. Stir-fry the garlic mixture until it begins to release strong aromas.

5 Add the meat and stir-fry over a high heat. Sprinkle with salt to taste.

6 Stir in the rice noodles. Add the oyster and fish sauces, sugar, vinegar, powdered stock and a little water and heat for 1 minute, stirring continuously. Lastly stir in the basil. Serve immediately.

Those who enjoy herbs might also enjoy a mixture of mint and lemon balm in place of the basil. Finely chop the herbs and stir into the noodles immediately before serving.

Sticky Rice Balls
with Pork Filling

Delicious little rice balls make Far Eastern dining a real treat.

The secret: the filling creates an original dish full of surprises

Ingredients

1 cup glutinous **rice**

¼ lb raw, unpeeled **shrimp**

2 **scallions**

5 canned **water chestnuts**

5 oz **ground pork**

1 **egg**

1 tablespoon **potato flour**

2 tablespoons **fish sauce**

pepper

2 tablespoons **vegetable oil**

Preparation
SERVES 4

1 Soak the glutinous rice for about 8 to 10 hours in lukewarm water, then pour off the water and cook for about 20 minutes in a steamer.

2 Wash, peel, and de-vein the shrimp. Chop finely.

3 Trim and wash the scallions and slice into fine rings. Chop the water chestnuts into small pieces.

4 Mix well together all ingredients except the rice.

5 To make the rice balls with a tablespoon scoop out 2 tablespoons of the rice and make into round, flat circles. Place 1 tablespoon of the meat mixture in the center of each circle and shape the rice around the filling to make small, equal-sized balls. Continue until all the ingredients are used up.

6 Brush the base of a bamboo steamer with oil and place the rice balls inside. Fill a wok with about half an inch of water and bring to the boil. Put the bamboo steamer in the wok and steam, covered, for about 15 minutes. Serve the sticky rice balls with chili sauce and vegetables.

Sticky rice is easy to prepare: soak the rice overnight and cook the day before. You can make a sweet version of this dish with a filling of raisins and nuts.

Stir-fried Rice
with Cashews

Sheer heaven in every mouthful; crunchy nuts, fresh peppers and aromatic
scallions transform everyday rice into an exceptional dish

Ingredients

salt

2 cups long-grain **rice**

1 small **red pepper**

1 small **yellow pepper**

1 small **green pepper**

¼ lb English **cucumber**

2 **scallions**

½ cup **cashews**

4 tablespoons **vegetable oil**

pepper

Preparation
SERVES 4

1 Bring about 1 quart of slightly salted water to the boil, add the
rice and stir once. Bring back to the boil and then simmer the rice,
covered, until tender, about 20 minutes. Leave the cooked rice
to cool.

2 Wash the peppers, cut in half lengthways and remove the seeds,
core, and internal membranes. Dice the peppers finely.

3 Wash the cucumber and cut into small dice. Trim and wash the
scallions and cut into fine strips.

4 Heat up a wok. Dry-fry the cashews, remove and set aside. Pour
the oil in the wok and heat. Add the peppers, cucumber and
onions and stir-fry briefly. Stir in the rice and nuts, and fry for a
further 3 minutes.

5 Season the fried rice with salt and pepper. Stir-fry for a further
2 minutes. Serve on warmed plates or in individual bowls.

**The fried rice tastes even nuttier if you
replace half of it with wild rice. Instead
of the cashews, peanuts or shelled,
halved almonds make a delicious addition.**

Egg Noodles
with Cabbage and Shiitake Mushrooms

Preparation
SERVES 4

1 Cook the egg noodles in boiling salted water until just tender, according to the package instructions. Strain in a colander, rinse in cold water and leave to drain thoroughly.

2 Cut the white cabbage into quarters, remove the core and cut the quarters crosswise into fine strips.

3 Peel the carrots and slice lengthways, then cut into fine strips. Wash and halve the mushrooms.

4 Heat up a wok, add half the oil and stir-fry the strips of cabbage and carrot over medium heat without browning. Take out the vegetables and keep warm. Heat up the rest of the oil in the wok and stir-fry the mushrooms over high heat until golden brown.

5 Put the vegetable strips and noodles into the wok. Mix together thoroughly and season with salt, pepper, Chinese five spice powder and soy sauce.

Ingredients

3 x 3-oz packages **ramen noodle soup**

salt

1 lb **white cabbage**

1 large **carrot**

½ lb **shiitake mushrooms**

4 tablespoons **peanut oil**

pepper

1 teaspoon **Chinese five spice powder**

4 tablespoons **soy sauce**

44

Ingredients

½ lb **bean thread noodles**

2 **carrots**

1 **yellow pepper**

1 medium-size **zucchini**

1 **red chili** · 1 clove **garlic**

4 tablespoons **sesame oil**

salt · **pepper** · 2 tablespoons **soy sauce**

1 tablespoon **oyster sauce**

1 cup **beansprouts**

1 tablespoon chopped fresh **cilantro leaves**

1 tablespoon **sesame seeds**

Bean Thread Noodles
with Vegetables and Sesame Seeds

Preparation
SERVES 4

1 Soak the bean thread noodles for about 10 minutes in lukewarm water.

2 Peel the carrots. Wash the pepper, core, cut in half lengthways, remove the seeds and internal membranes. Cut the carrots, pepper halves and zucchini into fine strips. Wash, seed and finely chop the chili. Peel the garlic cloves.

3 Heat 3 tablespoons of oil in a wok and fry the garlic cloves until golden brown. Remove, and stir-fry the vegetables without browning. Season with salt and pepper.

4 Drain the noodles. Cut into pieces with a pair of scissors and mix in with the vegetables. Add the soy sauce, oyster sauce, the remaining oil and the washed beansprouts. Sprinkle with the cilantro and sesame seeds before serving.

Indonesian-style Curry Rice
with Chicken Breast

A rice speciality to get hooked on: Curry, chicken and

lemongrass make simply perfect partners

Ingredients

½ lb boneless skinless
chicken breast

1 tablespoon **honey**

3 tablespoons **soy sauce**

2 tablespoons **curry powder**

1 tablespoon **ketchup**

1 teaspoon **cornstarch**

2 stalks **lemongrass**

1 bunch **scallions**

1 **red pepper**

2 cloves **garlic**

1 **red chili**

4 tablespoons **sesame oil**

4 cups cooked **basmati rice**

Preparation
SERVES 4

1 Rinse the chicken in cold water, pat dry and cut into fine strips.

2 Make a marinade by stirring together the honey, soy sauce,
   1 tablespoon of the curry powder, ketchup and cornstarch. Leave
   to stand for 15 minutes.

3 Wash the lemongrass, cut in half lengthways and slice into fine
   rings. Trim and wash the scallions and cut into ½ to ¾-inch long
   pieces. Prepare and wash the pepper and cut into small dice.

4 Peel the garlic and chop finely. Wash the chili, remove the seeds
   and cut into very fine strips.

5 Heat up a wok and add the oil. Stir-fry the meat. Add the onions,
   pepper and lemongrass and fry briefly with the meat. Stir in the
   garlic and chili. Add the cold rice and stir-fry together for about
   3 minutes. Finally add the remaining curry powder and give a good
   stir. Cook for 1 minute longer.

**Don't feel like meat? Curry rice can
transform a vegetarian meal if, instead
of chicken, bananas find their way into
the wok. In that case use only half the
marinade and stir-fry very briefly.**

Bean Thread Noodles
with Chicken and Vegetables

Noodles just like the Chinese like them: Experience the Far Eastern way of life
with tender chicken and an array of vegetables on the table

Ingredients

1 lb boneless skinless
chicken breasts

2 **green peppers**

4 **carrots**

¼ lb **celery root**

2 **scallions**

2 **red chilies**

6 tablespoons **sesame oil**

2 cups **chicken stock**

4 tablespoons **light soy sauce**

salt

pepper

½ lb **bean thread noodles**

a few fresh **cilantro leaves**

Preparation
SERVES 4

1 Cut the chicken into 1-inch pieces. Prepare and wash the pepper
and carrots and cut into fine strips. Peel the celery root and cut
into small dice. Trim and wash the scallions and cut into fine rings.
Wash and seed the chilies and chop finely.

2 Heat up a wok and put in 2 tablespoons of the oil. Lightly fry the
meat. Pour in the chicken stock and add the soy sauce. Leave the
meat to marinate for 15 minutes in the stock and then remove.

3 Next add the carrots to the stock and leave to simmer for
4 minutes. Repeat with the pepper, followed by the scallions.
Remove. Place the diced celery root and chilies in the stock and
cook for 5 minutes. Season to taste with salt and pepper.

4 Meanwhile cook the bean thread noodles according to the
instructions on the package, strain in a sieve, refresh with cold
water and leave to drain thoroughly.

5 Return the meat and vegetables to the soup, heat and serve with
the bean thread noodles. Drizzle with the rest of the sesame oil
and serve garnished with cilantro leaves.

**To achieve a sharper and more
refreshingly tangy flavor, add a stalk of
lemongrass cut into fine rings to the
stock at the same time as the celery root.**

Asian-style Noodle Soup
mit Shrimps und Mango

Always delicious: this fragrant soup of egg noodles, shrimp and
mango is an absolute must for all Asian food lovers

Ingredients

½ lb **Chinese egg noodles**

½ lb frozen **shrimp**

1 bunch **scallions**

1 ripe **mango**

1 tablespoon **corn oil**

⅔ cup **vegetable stock**

2½ tablespoons **soy sauce**

juice of 1 **lemon**

1 teaspoon **sambal oelek**

2 tablespoons **mango chutney**

salt · pepper

2 **limes**

3 tablespoons fresh chopped
chives

Preparation
SERVES 4

1 Cook the noodles until just tender, according to the packet
instructions. Strain in a colander, and leave to drain. Pour warm
water over the shrimp in a sieve and leave to drain.

2 Prepare and wash the scallions and cut into very fine strips about
2 inches long. Peel the mango and cut into cubes.

3 Heat up a wok and add the oil. Stir-fry the shrimp for 3 minutes.
Pour in the vegetable stock. Add the scallions and noodles and
leave to simmer for 5 minutes.

4 Season the stock with the soy sauce, lemon juice, sambal oelek,
mango chutney, salt and pepper. Leave to infuse for 10 minutes.

5 Wash and scrub the limes. Cut one of the limes into wedges and
set aside. With a zester cut fine strips of peel from the other lime.

6 Ladle the soup into individual bowls and pass the cubes of mango,
chives, wedges and zest of lime in separate bowls.

**Another variation on the Asian noodle
theme: Replace the shrimp with pieces of
boneless chicken breast. Add about
5 minutes to the cooking time of the soup.**

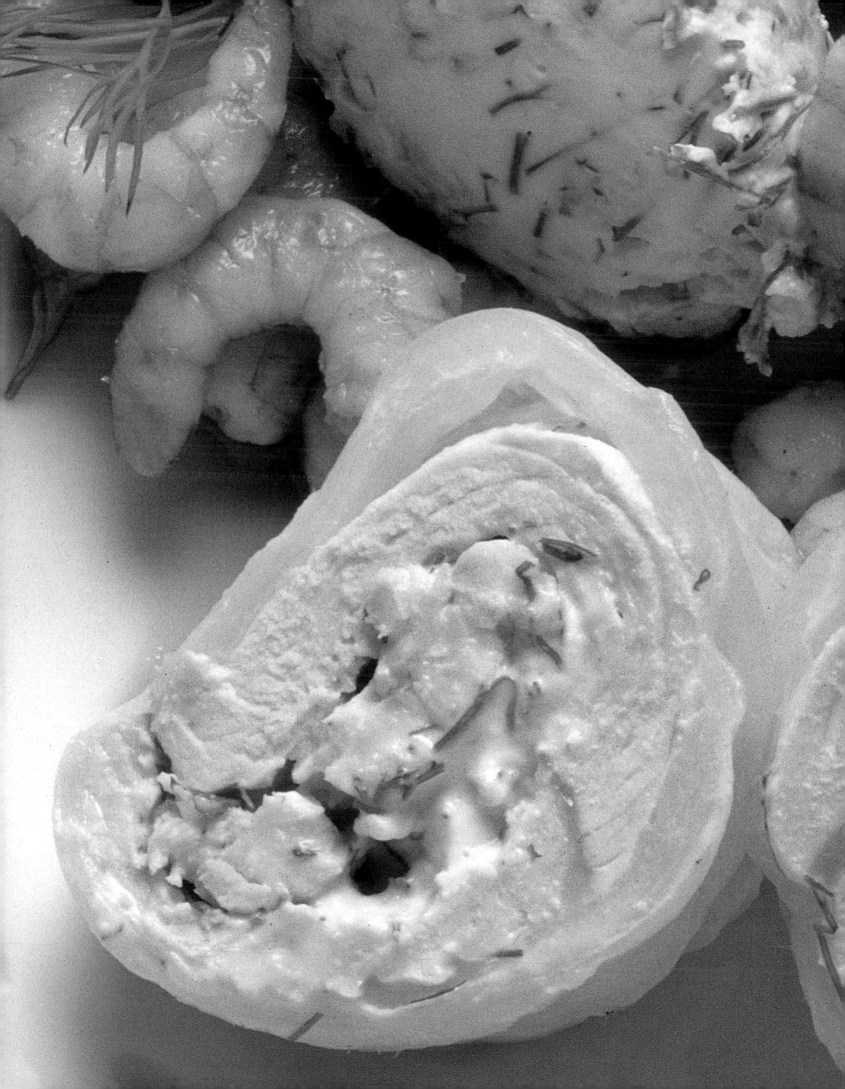

Meat &
poultry

Stir-fried Chicken
with Ginger and Rice

Fragrant basmati rice with a hint of ginger makes tender chicken breast and crunchy vegetables into a mouth-watering combination

Ingredients

2 cups **basmati rice** · **salt**

6 **scallions**

6 small **carrots**

1 lb boneless skinless **chicken breasts**

pepper

4 teaspoons **cornstarch**

4 tablespoons **vegetable oil**

2 cups **beansprouts**

1 teaspoon ground **ginger**

4 tablespoons **rice wine**

4 tablespoons **soy sauce**

Preparation
SERVES 4

1 Wash the rice thoroughly in a sieve under the tap and bring to the boil in twice its volume of water. Season with salt, cover and simmer over a low heat.

2 Wash and prepare the scallions and cut into fine rings. Peel the carrots, cut in half lengthways and chop into reasonably large pieces.

3 Cut the chicken breast diagonally into thin slices. Season with salt and pepper and dust with cornstarch.

4 Heat up a wok and add the oil. Brown the chicken, stirring constantly, remove and set aside in a warm place. Add the scallions, carrots and washed beansprouts to the wok and cook for 5 minutes, stirring from time to time. Season with ginger, rice wine and soy sauce. Bring to the boil and add salt and pepper to taste.

5 Spoon the vegetables on to plates, arrange the chicken pieces on top and serve with the basmati rice.

Ginger has a characteristic, slightly pungent aroma. Its essential oils stimulate the digestion and strengthen the immune system. Fresh ginger tastes stronger and flavors a dish more noticeably than ground ginger.

Breast of Duck
with Cilantro Noodles

Fancy something exotic? Tender duck breast, honey and

spicy cilantro provide real gastronomic delights for poultry lovers

Ingredients

¾ lb **Chinese egg noodles**

salt

1 ¼ lbs **duck breast**

1 tablespoon **honey**

4 tablespoons **soy sauce**

½ teaspoon **sambal oelek**

1 **red pepper**

1 bunch **scallions**

3 tablespoons **vegetable oil**

2 tablespoons **lemon juice**

1 cup **chicken stock**

2 tablespoons chopped fresh **cilantro leaves**

Preparation
SERVES 4

1 Cook the noodles in salted water according to the package instructions, strain in a colander, rinse in cold water and leave to drain well.

2 Cut the duck breast into thin slices. Stir the honey together with the soy sauce and sambal oelek. Stir in the meat and marinate for 30 minutes.

3 Core and halve the red pepper and remove the seeds and internal membranes. Wash the halves, then cut into fine strips.

4 Wash and trim the scallions. Cut the green part into rings and the white part into fine strips.

5 Take the meat out of the marinade and leave to drain, reserving the marinade. Stir-fry the duck breast in 1 tablespoon of the oil in a hot wok over high heat, then remove. Fry the red pepper and scallions in the wok in the rest of the oil until just tender. Sprinkle over salt and lemon juice to season, and pour in the stock and reserved marinade. Add the duck breast and noodles, bring up to the boil and serve sprinkled with the cilantro.

**You can also use boneless turkey or chicken breasts instead of the duck breast.
If using turkey or chicken, spice up the marinade with an additional 2 tablespoons lime juice and 1 teaspoon honey.**

Turkey Curry
with Coconut Milk

Discover the magic of Thai cuisine! Creamy coconut milk and
yellow curry paste combine with meat and vegetables in perfect harmony

Ingredients

1 ¼ lbs **turkey breast**

1 **red pepper**

½ lb **scallions**

1 large bunch fresh **basil**

1 ⅔ cups unsweetened
coconut milk

1 tablespoon **yellow curry paste**

2 tablespoons **soy sauce**

1 tablespoon **sugar**

Preparation
SERVES 4

1 Wash the turkey breast and pat dry. With a sharp kitchen knife
first cut into ½-inch thick pieces and then into fine strips.

2 Core and halve the red pepper lengthways and remove the seeds
and internal membranes. Wash the halves and cut into fine strips.
Wash and prepare the scallions and cut into ½-inch thick rings.
Wash the basil and shake dry. Pick the leaves off the stems. Finely
chop half the leaves and reserve the rest for decoration.

3 Bring the coconut milk to the boil in a wok, stir in the curry paste
and simmer for 1 minute. Add the strips of turkey breast and
simmer for a further 4 minutes, stirring from time to time.

4 Add the prepared vegetables and simmer everything together for
a further 3 minutes. Stir in enough chopped basil, soy sauce
and sugar to taste. Serve the curry with the reserved basil leaves.

**The fine, refreshing aroma of the fresh
basil leaves is even further enhanced if
they are deep-fried separately in hot oil
for 1 minute before serving.**

Turkey Rolls
with a Shrimp and Dill Filling

Preparation
SERVES 4

1 Mix the rice wine and soy sauce together and marinate the turkey escalopes for about 30 minutes.

2 Blanch the Chinese cabbage leaves briefly in boiling salted water, plunge into ice cold water and then leave to drain in a sieve.

3 Cut the shrimp into small pieces, season with lemon juice and ginger and mix together with the dill and cream cheese. Divide equally between the marinated slices of meat.

4 Place the escalopes on the Chinese cabbage leaves and fold in the long edges. Roll up the Chinese leaves from the short edge and place in a bamboo basket or steamer.

5 Bring half an inch of water to the boil in a wok. Put in the bamboo basket or steamer and cook the turkey rolls in the steam, covered, for about 5 minutes. Take out of the bamboo basket or steamer and serve with soy sauce.

Ingredients

4 tablespoons **rice wine**

1 tablespoon **soy sauce**

½ lb **turkey escalopes** (4 total)

4 **Chinese cabbage leaves**

salt

⅓ lb peeled **shrimp**

1 teaspoon **lemon juice**

¼ teaspoon grated fresh **ginger**

1 tablespoon chopped fresh **dill**

⅓ cup full-fat **cream cheese**

Ingredients

8 large **Swiss chard leaves**

salt

1 **shallot**

1 tablespoon **capers**

2–3 sprigs **parsley**

6-oz can **tuna fish**

1 tablespoon **crème fraîche**
or sour cream

pepper

½ lb **turkey escalopes** (4 total)

Turkey Rolls
with Tuna Fish Filling

Preparation
SERVES 4

1 Blanch the Swiss chard leaves in boiling salted water, plunge into ice cold water and leave to drain thoroughly.

2 Peel the shallots and chop finely. Likewise chop the capers into very small pieces. Wash and finely chop the parsley.

3 Separate the tuna fish into small flakes with a fork and mix with the onions, capers, chopped parsley and crème fraîche. Season with salt and pepper.

4 Place 2 Swiss chard leaves on top of each other. Lay the turkey escalopes on the leaves and spread them with a thin layer of the tuna fish mixture. Fold in the long edges, roll up the Swiss chard leaves from the short edge and place in a bamboo basket or steamer.

5 Bring half an inch of water to the boil in a wok. Put in the bamboo basket and steam the turkey rolls, covered, for 5 minutes.

Chicken Fritters
with Sesame Seeds and Vegetables

Lovely and crispy: These spicy pieces of chicken are wrapped
in a paper thin coating of delicately crunchy batter and sesame seeds

Ingredients

1 egg white · 1 cup flour

3 tablespoons cornstarch

2 teaspoons baking powder

salt · pepper

1 cup water

½ cup vegetable oil

1 teaspoon grated fresh ginger

7 tablespoons soy sauce

5 tablespoons rice wine

1 lb boneless skinless
chicken breasts

4 medium carrots

2 bunches scallions

½ lb mung beansprouts

2 tablespoons sesame seeds

oil for deep-frying

Preparation
SERVES 4

1 Mix together the flour, cornstarch, baking powder, salt and pepper
in a small bowl. To make the batter, whisk the egg white until stiff.
Fold the flour mixture a spoonful at a time into the egg white,
alternating with the water. Stir in 6 tablespoons of the oil. Leave
the batter to stand for 30 minutes.

2 Mix the ginger with 2 tablespoons each of the soy sauce and the
rice wine. Drizzle over the meat, cover, and set to one side.

3 Peel the carrots and cut into strips. Trim and wash the scallions and
cut on the slant into slices. Wash the beansprouts and leave to drain.

4 Heat a wok and add 2 tablespoons of the remaining oil. Stir-fry
the carrots and scallions. Pour in the rest of the soy sauce, rice
wine and 3 tablespoons water, and leave to cook for 5 minutes.
Fold in the beansprouts, heat briefly and season to taste. Set the
vegetables aside and keep warm.

5 Clean the wok and heat the oil for deep-frying. Fold the sesame
seeds into the batter. Dip the pieces of chicken in the batter and
fry individually in the hot fat for about 3 minutes each, lift out
and drain on paper towels. Serve with the vegetables.

**This batter is also suitable for other white
meats, such as turkey or veal. You can
also make delicious fritters in this way with
pieces of fish or blanched vegetables.**

Chicken
with Morel Mushrooms

This chicken recipe is typically Chinese: the combination of morel mushrooms,
leeks and carrots makes it an all-time favorite of fans of Oriental food

Ingredients

12 dried **morel mushrooms**

1 clove **garlic**

1 **green chili**

1 ¼ lbs boneless skinless
chicken breast

1 tablespoon **cornstarch**

4 tablespoons **soy sauce**

½ cup **rice wine**

1 tablespoon grated fresh **ginger**

1 **leek** · 5 medium **carrots**

1 small head **cauliflower**

6 tablespoons **corn oil**

2 cups **beansprouts**

salt · **pepper**

1 tablespoon chopped fresh
cilantro leaves

Preparation
SERVES 4

1   Leave the morel mushrooms to soak for 30 minutes in warm water.
Peel the garlic, wash and seed the chili. Finely chop the garlic
and chili.

2   Cut the chicken breast into strips. Whisk the cornstarch, soy sauce
and rice wine together, add the ginger, chili and garlic, and use to
marinate the meat for 30 minutes.

3   Wash and prepare the vegetables. Cut the leek into rings, the
carrots into strips, and separate the cauliflower into small florets.

4   Heat a wok and add 1 tablespoon of the oil. Lift the chicken out
of the marinade, leave for a moment to drain, and fry in small
portions over high heat, then remove.

5   Heat up the rest of the oil in the wok and cook the leeks, carrots
and cauliflower a little at a time until just tender. Add the morel
mushrooms, washed beansprouts and meat. Add the marinade, salt
and pepper, simmer briefly and stir in the cilantro.

**Dried morel mushrooms have a very
strong taste. However, other mushrooms
can easily be substituted for them,
such as fresh shiitake mushrooms, or a
domestic variety.**

Chicken and Vegetables
with Bean Thread Noodles

Preparation
SERVES 4

1 Wash the chicken breasts, pat dry and cut into narrow strips. Mix with the soy sauce and leave to marinate for 30 minutes.

2 Heat the oven to 450°F. Cut the peppers in half lengthways and remove the seeds, core, and internal membranes. Wash the halves, and roast in the oven, cut-side down until the skin turns brown and blisters. Leave to cool under a kitchen towel, pull off the skin and cut the peppers into narrow strips.

3 Clean the mushrooms and slice thinly. Wash the snow peas. Rinse the Chinese cabbage leaves and cut into strips. Wash the beansprouts and leave to drain.

4 Heat 2 tablespoons of the oil in a wok and stir-fry the vegetables over a high heat. Season with salt, lift out and set aside in a warm place. Dust the chicken strips with cornstarch and fry over a very high heat in the rest of the oil. Mix in the curry paste, ginger and cilantro. Add the noodles and chicken stock. Simmer for 2 minutes.

Ingredients

4 boneless skinless **chicken breasts**

2 tablespoons **soy sauce**

1 each of **red**, **yellow** and **green peppers**

¼ lb **shiitake mushrooms** · ¼ lb **snow peas**

½ lb **Chinese cabbage leaves**

1 ½ cups **beansprouts**

4 tablespoons **sesame oil**

1 tablespoon **cornstarch** · **salt**

½ tablespoon **red curry paste**

1 tablespoon grated fresh **ginger**

1 tablespoon chopped fresh **cilantro leaves**

¼ lb cooked **bean thread noodles**

⅓ cup **chicken stock**

Ingredients

¾ lb **beef tenderloin**

5 tablespoons **soy sauce**

1 tablespoon dried **tree ear mushrooms**

6 **scallions** · 1 **carrot**

¼ lb each small **mushrooms** and **snow peas**

¼ lb **baby corncobs**

¼ lb **French green beans**

2 cloves **garlic** · 2 dried **chilies**

6 tablespoons **sesame oil**

1 teaspoon grated **fresh ginger**

salt · **pepper** · 2 tablespoons **dry sherry**

¼ cup **vegetable stock**

Stir-fried Beef
with Vegetables and Chili

Preparation
SERVES 4

1 Cut the beef into very fine strips, combine with the soy sauce and leave to marinate for 30 minutes.

2 Pour boiling water over the mushrooms and soak according to the instructions on the package, then cut into small pieces. Wash the vegetables, and cut finely.

3 Wash the snow peas, baby corncobs and beans. Blanch the beans for 1 minute, then refresh with cold water.

4 Peel the garlic and chop finely. Crush the chilies finely.

5 Heat 4 tablespoons of the oil in a wok. Cook the chili, garlic and ginger. Add the carrots, beans, corn, mushrooms and scallions one after the other, cooking for 1 minute after each addition, until just tender. Remove, and keep warm. Stir-fry the meat in the remaining oil over a high heat, then mix with the vegetables. Add salt, pepper, soy sauce, sherry and stock and bring to the boil.

Asian-style Salad
with Radish and Papaya

Light and crunchy: the beansprouts and nuts in this Asian snack
make it an ideal treat for any break, guaranteed to lift the spirits

Ingredients

½ lb **pork escalopes**

1 **carrot** · ½ **green papaya**

¼ lb **radishes** · 1 English **cucumber**

½ stalk **lemongrass** · 3 **red chilies**

1 tablespoon **peanuts**

4 tablespoons **peanut oil**

2 ½ cups **beansprouts**

1 tablespoon **honey**

1 tablespoon each of **soy sauce**
and **fish sauce**

6 tablespoons **lemon juice**

salt · **pepper**

1 tablespoon chopped fresh
cilantro leaves

Preparation
SERVES 4

1 Using a sharp kitchen knife cut the pork escalopes across the grain into thin strips.

2 Peel the carrots and cut into matchstick pieces. Seed the papaya, peel the radish, and cut both into strips. Wash the cucumber, cut in half and remove the seeds. Cut into thin strips. Trim and wash the lemongrass and chilies, and cut both into fine rings.

3 Heat a wok and dry-roast the peanuts until golden brown. Cool for a moment and then chop.

4 Heat half the oil in the wok, add the sliced pork, stir-fry on all sides for about 5 minutes, take out of the wok and leave to cool. Put the carrot sticks, washed beansprouts, chili and lemongrass in the wok and cook for about 2 minutes, then leave to cool.

5 Stir together the honey, the rest of the oil, the soy sauce, fish sauce, lemon juice, salt and pepper. Mix with the meat and the rest of the ingredients.

Fresh pineapple instead of papaya and boneless chicken breast instead of pork make a deliciously fruity version of this Asian salad. Just add a level teaspoon of sugar to the marinade.

Sweet and sour Pork
with Pineapple and Tomatoes

Not only a big favorite in China: the abundance of typical ingredients
makes this classic specialty simply irresistible

Ingredients

1 ½ lbs **pork tenderloin**

1-inch piece fresh **ginger**

4 cloves **garlic** · 3 **red chilies**

½ lb **tomatoes**

1 lb fresh **pineapple**

2 tablespoons **sesame oil**

2 tablespoons **corn oil**

4 tablespoons **rice vinegar**

4 tablespoons light **soy sauce**

4 teaspoons **sherry**

2 tablespoons **sugar**

1 cup **chicken stock**

2 teaspoons **cornstarch**

Preparation
SERVES 4

1 Rinse the pork in cold water, pat dry and cut into equal-sized thin
strips.

2 Peel the ginger and slice very thinly. Peel the garlic and chop
finely. Wash the chilies, remove the seeds and cut into very fine
strips.

3 Immerse the tomatoes in boiling water, skin them, cut in half,
remove the seeds and cut into dice. Peel the pineapple, remove
the core and cut the flesh into ½-inch chunks.

4 Heat a wok and add the sesame oil and corn oil. Stir-fry the meat.
Add the ginger, garlic, and chilies and briefly stir-fry together.
Add the tomatoes and pineapple and stir-fry 1 to 2 minutes longer.
Add the vinegar, soy sauce, sherry and sugar. Pour in ¾ cup of the
stock and mix well.

5 Stir the cornstarch into the rest of the stock and pour evenly over
the meat. Combine thoroughly and leave everything to simmer for
about 3 minutes.

**There are many different varieties of soy sauce
with many different flavor characteristics.
As a general guide: Indonesian and Thai varieties
are somewhat sweet, Japanese is salty, and
Chinese soy sauce is slightly bitter.**

Stir-fried Beef
with Vegetables and Sherry

Preparation
SERVES 4

1 Prepare and wash the vegetables. Slice the carrots, leeks and celery sticks finely, and cut the pepper into fine strips.

2 Using a sharp kitchen knife cut the rump steak across the grain into strips about ½-inch wide.

3 Heat a wok and add the oil. Over a high heat stir-fry the strips of meat for about 5 minutes. Take out the meat and keep warm.

4 Reduce the heat and gradually stir-fry the vegetables in the wok in batches. Add the sherry, mix in the peas and season with the soy sauce, salt, pepper, curry powder and Hoisin sauce.

5 Cook the vegetables for about 2 more minutes, then season generously with salt and pepper. Finally stir in the beef strips and chopped parsley. If you wish serve the stir-fried beef with basmati rice.

Ingredients

1 lb **carrots** · ½ lb **leeks**

1 stalk **celery**

1 **red pepper**

½ lb **rump steak**

3 tablespoons **vegetable oil** · ½ cup **sherry**

⅔ cup frozen **peas**

2 tablespoons **soy sauce**

salt · **pepper** · 1 tablespoon **curry powder**

1 teaspoon **Hoisin sauce**

1 tablespoon chopped fresh **parsley**

Ingredients

1 lb **Savoy cabbage**

½ lb **shiitake mushrooms**

1 small **onion**

2 cloves **garlic**

1 lb **pork tenderloin**

salt · pepper

3 tablespoons **vegetable oil**

1 teaspoon grated fresh **ginger**

1 tablespoon **curry powder**

6 tablespoons **beef** or **chicken stock**

3 tablespoons **soy sauce**

1 tablespoon chopped fresh **parsley**

Pork Tenderloin
with Savoy Cabbage and Mushrooms

Preparation
SERVES 4

1 Halve the Savoy cabbage, remove the outer leaves and core. Wash the halves and cut into thin strips. Clean the mushrooms and slice thinly. Peel the onion and the garlic and finely chop both.

2 With a sharp kitchen knife cut the meat across the grain first into slices and then into strips. Season with salt and pepper.

3 Heat the oil in a wok and stir-fry the meat over high heat. Remove the meat from the wok and keep warm.

4 Reduce the heat and stir-fry the cabbage, onions, garlic and mushrooms in batches. Season with ginger, curry powder and pepper, then pour in the stock and soy sauce. Briefly bring to the boil. Lastly stir in the meat and parsley and heat through.

Lamb Curry
with Coconut and Lime Sauce

A classic dish made with tender pieces of lamb: Indulge the senses with fragrant spices
and a smooth, creamy coconut milk sauce

Ingredients

1 ½ lbs **lamb** (cut from the leg)

1 **lemon**

2 teaspoons **sambal oelek**

2 teaspoons **sugar**

1 teaspoon ground **coriander**

1 teaspoon **cinnamon**

salt · pepper

2 stalks **lemongrass**

1-inch piece fresh **ginger**

3 cloves **garlic** · 3 **shallots**

4 tablespoons **vegetable oil**

2 teaspoons **turmeric**

1 teaspoon **curry powder**

1 ⅔ cups unsweetened **coconut milk**

2 sprigs fresh **cilantro**

Preparation
SERVES 4

1 Rinse the lamb in cold water, pat dry and cut evenly into thin
strips.

2 Scrub the lemon under hot running water, wipe dry and grate the
rind. Cut the lemon in half and juice it. Mix the lemon juice,
rind, sambal oelek, sugar, coriander, cinnamon, salt and pepper
together to make a marinade and stir into the meat.

3 Wash the lemongrass, cut in half lengthways and then into strips.
Peel the ginger and slice very finely. Peel the garlic and shallots
and chop very finely.

4 Heat a wok and add the oil. Briefly stir-fry the garlic, shallots,
ginger and lemongrass. Add the meat and stir-fry. Sprinkle over
the turmeric and curry powder and cook for 2 minutes. Stir in the
coconut milk and leave everything to simmer for 5 minutes.

5 Wash the fresh cilantro, pat dry and pick the leaves off the stems.
Garnish the lamb curry with the cilantro according to taste and
serve with basmati rice.

**In the late spring lamb has a particularly
fine flavor. The first shoots of grass
and the mother's milk give the meat an
exceptional quality.**

Fish &
Seafood

Rice Noodles
with Seafood

The best possible combination: Shrimp, squid, mussels and

Thai basil come together to create a Thai-style noodle extravaganza

Ingredients

½ lb **rice sticks**

¼ lb raw, unpeeled **shrimp**

¼ lb **squid**, tentacles removed

1 large **onion**

3 each of **red** and **green chilies**

3 sprigs Thai or ordinary **basil**

3 cloves **garlic**

3 tablespoons **vegetable oil**

¼ lb **clams**, shelled

2 tablespoons **oyster sauce**

2 tablespoons **fish sauce**

Preparation
SERVES 4

1 Leave the rice noodles to soak for 10 minutes in lukewarm water. Strain in a sieve and cut into 2-inch lengths with a pair of scissors.

2 Wash, peel and de-vein the shrimp. Wash the squid thoroughly and cut into strips.

3 Peel the onion, wash and seed the chilies. Cut the onion and chili into fine strips. Wash the basil and pat dry. Pick off the leaves and tear into pieces. Peel and finely chop the garlic.

4 Heat a wok and add the oil. Soften the garlic over a medium heat. Add the seafood and stir. Flavor to taste with oyster and fish sauces.

5 Add the drained noodles and stir-fry together for 3 minutes. Lastly add the basil, chili and onion strips. Mix everything well together and cook for a further 3 minutes.

The piquancy of this dish makes it an ideal meal for a hot summer's day. For a milder taste replace the chili with a stalk of finely chopped lemongrass.

Fish Curry
with Spicy Rice

A perfect balance of spices: The cloves, cinnamon and saffron in this fish curry
are sure to inspire even the most discriminating of gourmets

Ingredients

1 ½ cups **basmati rice**

3 **cloves** · 1 stick **cinnamon**

1 teaspoon **cardamom**

1 ¼ lbs **cod fillets**

2 **shallots**

2 cloves **garlic**

2 teaspoons grated fresh **ginger**

2 sprigs **cilantro**

2 tablespoons **sesame oil**

4 tablespoons **soy sauce**

6 tablespoons unsweetened
coconut milk

2 teaspoons **curry powder**

1 teaspoon **chili powder**

1 pinch **saffron threads**

1 tablespoon **ground almonds**

1 tablespoon **lemon juice**

salt · pepper

Preparation
SERVES 4

1 Wash the rice thoroughly under running water, and bring to the
boil with the cloves, cinnamon and cardamom in twice its volume
of water. Simmer until tender, covered, about 20 minutes.

2 Wash the fish, pat dry and cut into bite-size pieces.

3 Peel and finely chop the shallots and garlic. Peel the ginger and
grate finely. Wash the cilantro and pat dry. Pick off the leaves and
roughly chop.

4 Heat a wok and add the oil. Stir-fry the shallots. Add the garlic
and grated ginger and continue to stir-fry briefly.

5 Pour in the soy sauce and coconut milk. Stir in the curry powder,
chili powder, saffron, almonds and lemon juice and season to taste
with salt and pepper.

6 Add the pieces of fish to the sauce and simmer over a medium
heat for about 4 minutes, stirring occasionally. Lastly add the
chopped cilantro and serve the fish curry with the spicy rice.

Monkfish
with Savoy Cabbage and Lentils

Preparation
SERVES 4

1 Halve the cabbage and cut away the core. Cut the leaves into strips about ½-inch wide. Halve the pepper lengthways, core, and remove the seeds. Wash the two halves and cut into small dice.

2 Cut the fish into bite-size pieces, season with salt and pepper. Beat the egg white until slightly frothy and stir in the cornstarch. Dip the pieces of fish first in the egg white and then in the sesame seeds. Press the coating firmly onto the pieces of fish.

3 Heat a wok and add the oil. Stir-fry the fish pieces on all sides for 3 minutes. Remove and set aside in a warm place.

4 Place the vegetables in the oil and cook over a medium heat for about 6 minutes, stirring from time to time. Season with the curry powder and nutmeg. Pour over the sherry, lobster or fish stock and vinegar and boil briefly. Stir in the lentils and return to a boil. Spoon the fish on top of the vegetables and garnish with the chervil leaves before serving.

Ingredients

¾ lb **Savoy cabbage** · 1 **red pepper**

1 ¼ lbs **monkfish fillets**

salt · **pepper**

2 **egg whites** · 2 tablespoons **cornstarch**

½ cup **sesame seeds**

6 tablespoons **vegetable oil**

1 teaspoon **curry powder** · 1 pinch **nutmeg**

4 tablespoons **sherry**

½ cup **lobster** or **fish stock**

1 tablespoon **sherry vinegar**

½ cup cooked **green lentils**

1 tablespoon fresh **chervil leaves**

Ingredients

½ lb each of white fish fillets and shrimp

salt · pepper · 4 tablespoons lemon juice

2 sticks celery · 2 small zucchini

1 red pepper · 4 scallions

¼ lb shiitake mushrooms

⅓ cup vegetable oil

3 tablespoons sherry

1 tablespoon cornstarch

1 teaspoon curry powder

1 pinch each of ground ginger and coriander

3 tablespoons soy sauce

6 tablespoons fish stock

Stir-fried Fish
with Vegetables and Sherry

Preparation
SERVES 4

1 Cut the fish into bite-size pieces, then season fish and shrimp with salt and pepper and sprinkle with lemon juice.

2 Wash and prepare the vegetables. Cut into slices, strips or cubes.

3 Heat the oil in a wok until very hot. Over a very high heat stir-fry the fish and shrimp for about 3 minutes. Lift out, cover and keep in a warm place.

4 Place the vegetables in the wok and cook for about 6 to 8 minutes until just tender. Pour in the sherry.

5 Mix the cornstarch and the spices together and stir into the soy sauce and fish stock until smooth. Pour this mixture over the vegetables and simmer for 3 minutes.

6 Stir the fish and shrimp into the vegetables and return to a boil. Boil for 1 minute, then remove from the heat.

Fish Nuggets
with Vegetable Rice

Small but delicate: Fish nuggets in a crispy coating, quick and
simple to prepare with a delight in every bite

Ingredients

2 cups **basmati rice**

1 bunch **cilantro**

¼ lb each of **broccoli** and **carrots**

½ cup **beansprouts**

1 lb **white fish fillet**,
such as cod or hake

6 tablespoons **lemon juice**

salt · pepper

flour for coating

2 **eggs**

1 tablespoon **sesame oil**

1 teaspoon fresh grated **ginger**

oil for deep-frying

Preparation
SERVES 4

1 Put the rice in a sieve and rinse with cold water, then bring to a
   boil in twice its volume of water, add salt, cover and leave to
   simmer over a low heat until tender, about 20 minutes. Wash the
   cilantro, shake dry, roughly chop and mix into the cooked rice.

2 Wash the broccoli and peel the carrots. Separate the broccoli into
   small florets. Cut the carrots into quarters lengthways and then
   into small pieces. Wash the beansprouts and leave to drain.

3 Cut the fish into bite-size strips, sprinkle with lemon juice. Leave
   to marinate for 5 minutes, then season with salt and pepper.
   Sprinkle some flour onto a flat plate. Beat the eggs in a second
   dish with 1 teaspoon water.

4 Heat a wok and add the oil. Stir-fry the vegetables for about
   5 minutes. Mix in the beansprouts and ginger and season with salt
   and pepper. Fold the mixed vegetables into the cooked rice.

5 Clean the wok, pour in enough oil for deep-frying and heat. Toss
   the fish strips in flour, dip in the egg and fry in the hot oil until
   golden brown. Serve on top of the vegetable rice.

**A tangy apricot dip makes an excellent
accompaniment: stir 3 tablespoons soy sauce,
1 teaspoon sambal oelek, 1 tablespoon lemon
juice and 4 tablespoons apricot jam together and
season to taste with 1 pinch of ground ginger.**

Sweet and sour Fish Stew
with Ginger and Bamboo Shoots

Preparation
SERVES 4

1 Cut the fish into bite-size pieces.

2 Peel the ginger and garlic and chop finely. Trim and wash the scallions and cut into very fine strips. Rinse and drain the bamboo shoots in a sieve. Clean the mushrooms and slice thinly.

3 Heat a wok, add the oil and stir-fry the pieces of fish. Remove and keep in a warm place.

4 Put the ginger and garlic into the wok and stir-fry briefly. Add the mushrooms and cook for about 3 minutes over a medium heat, stirring from time to time. Stir in the mango chutney, vinegar, sherry, soy sauce, sugar and stock.

5 Mix in the fish pieces carefully. Blend the cornstarch with 2 tablespoons water in a small bowl, pour over the fish and stir in quickly and evenly. Let the fish stew simmer for a further 2 minutes, then add salt and pepper to taste and serve.

Ingredients

1 ¼ lbs **mixed fish fillets**, such as cod, hake, or salmon

2 tablespoons fresh grated **ginger**

2 cloves **garlic** · 2 **scallions**

6-oz can **bamboo shoots**

1 cup small **mushrooms**

3 tablespoons **corn oil**

4 tablespoons **mango chutney**

⅓ cup **rice vinegar** · 4 teaspoons **sherry**

4 tablespoons **soy sauce** · 2 tablespoons **sugar**

6 tablespoons **vegetable stock**

1 teaspoon **cornstarch**

Ingredients

4-oz can **hearts of palm**

1 **yellow pepper** · 3 **scallions**

2 teaspoons grated fresh **ginger**

3 cloves **garlic**

1 lb **sea bass fillets**

2 ½ teaspoons **tapioca starch**

salt · 3 tablespoons **rice wine**

⅓ cup drained canned **plum tomatoes**

1 tablespoon **brown sugar**

2 tablespoons **rice vinegar**

1 tablespoon **soy sauce**

4 tablespoons **peanut oil**

Sea Bass
in Red Sauce

Preparation
SERVES 4

1 Drain the hearts of palm in a sieve and cut into slices. Cut the pepper in half, core, and remove the seeds and internal membranes. Wash the pepper halves and cut into fine strips. Trim and wash the scallions and cut into rings. Peel and chop the ginger and garlic. Cut the fish into strips.

2 Stir 2 teaspoons of the tapioca starch with 1 tablespoon of water, salt and 1 tablespoon of rice wine. Marinate the strips of fish for 10 minutes.

3 Stir the tomatoes, sugar, vinegar and 2 tablespoons rice wine with 4 tablespoons water, and blend with the remaining tapioca starch and the soy sauce.

4 Heat the oil in a wok, drain the marinated pieces of fish and stir-fry until golden brown. Remove and keep warm. Cook the pepper, onions, ginger and garlic for 4 minutes, stirring occasionally. Add the hearts of palm and sauce and simmer for 2 minutes. Stir in the fish and heat through.

Jumbo Shrimp
with Mushrooms

Fine shrimp and fresh mushrooms: If Neptune had been

a gourmet this might have been his favorite dish

Ingredients

1 ¼ lbs large **shrimp**, peeled

4 **scallions**

½ lb small **mushrooms**

3 sprigs **cilantro**

3 tablespoons **vegetable oil**

1 teaspoon **chili powder**

1 tablespoon **cornstarch**

1 teaspoon **tomato paste**

1 teaspoon **sugar**

2 teaspoons **ground ginger**

salt · pepper

8 large **iceberg lettuce leaves**

Preparation
SERVES 4

1 Rinse the shrimp in cold water in a sieve, drain and pat dry with paper towels.

2 Trim and wash the scallions and cut into rings. Clean the mushrooms and cut in half. Wash the cilantro, pat dry and pick the leaves from the stems.

3 Heat a wok and add 2 tablespoons of the oil. Stir-fry the vegetables for about 2 minutes over a high heat. Push the vegetables to the edge of the wok, add the remaining oil and add the chili powder. Cook for 1 minute. Add the shrimp and stir to coat well with the chili powder. Stir-fry for 2 minutes.

4 Combine the cornstarch with 6 tablespoons water and the tomato paste and pour over the shrimp. Add the sugar and ground ginger. Stir in the mushrooms and scallions and leave to cook for about 1 minute. Season to taste with salt and pepper.

5 Arrange 2 lettuce leaves on each of 4 plates, fill with the shrimp mixture and garnish with the cilantro leaves.

A sweet and sour version of this recipe, omitting the hot ginger, also tastes delicious. Use 2 tablespoons tamarind pulp and 1 tablespoon palm sugar in place of the ginger.

Sweet and sour Shrimp
with Peppers

Preparation
SERVES 4

1 Beat the egg white until slightly frothy and stir in the vinegar, rice wine, soy sauce and ketchup to make a marinade, then season with salt and pepper. Rinse the shrimp in cold water, dry with paper towels, then marinate in the sauce for 20 minutes.

2 Cut the peppers in half lengthways, core, remove the seeds and internal membranes. Wash the pepper halves and cut into ¾-inch dice. Trim and wash the scallions and cut into rings. Wash and seed the chili and chop finely.

3 Take the shrimp out of the marinade, drain and dust with cornstarch.

4 Heat the oil in a wok and stir-fry the shrimp. Remove, and keep warm.

5 Over a medium heat stir-fry the vegetables for about 5 minutes. Season with ginger and add the marinade and lobster or fish stock. Simmer for 3 minutes and stir in the shrimp. Re-heat briefly.

Ingredients

1 **egg white**

2 tablespoons **balsamic vinegar**

4 tablespoons **rice wine**

2 tablespoons **soy sauce**

1 tablespoon **ketchup**

salt · pepper

20 large peeled **shrimp**

2 **red peppers** · 4 **scallions**

1 **red chili**

2 tablespoons **cornstarch**

½ cup **vegetable oil** · 1 pinch **ground ginger**

4 tablespoons **lobster** or **fish stock**

Ingredients

1 **lemon**

2 cloves **garlic**

1 **chili**

4 tablespoons **olive oil**

salt · pepper

24 jumbo **shrimp**

6 sheets **rice paper**

1 **egg white**

oil for deep-frying

a few **Chinese cabbage leaves**

Scampi
in Rice Paper Parcels

Preparation
SERVES 4

1 Halve the lemon and juice it. Peel the garlic and chop finely. Wash the chili, remove the seeds and also chop finely.

2 To make a marinade combine the lemon juice with the garlic, olive oil, chili, salt and pepper in a bowl. Stir the shrimp into the marinade. Leave to marinate for several hours in the refrigerator.

3 Soften the rice paper between wet tea towels. Cut each one into four and brush the edges with beaten egg white. Wrap one shrimp in each piece.

4 Heat up plenty of oil in a wok until it is very hot and deep-fry the shrimp parcels for about 4 minutes until golden brown. Arrange on the Chinese cabbage leaves and serve if you like with a sweet and spicy chili sauce.

Stir-fried Shrimp
with Hot Beansprouts

This dish has that fiery tang loved by Orientals: Shrimp, beansprouts
and sambal oelek make one's mouth water

Ingredients

¾ lb **Chinese egg noodles**

salt

1 bunch **scallions**

1 clove **garlic**

½ cup **beansprouts**

3 tablespoons **vegetable oil**

16 large **shrimp**, peeled

2 teaspoons **cornstarch**

1 cup **vegetable stock**

½ teaspoon **sambal oelek**

1 teaspoon **sugar**

1 tablespoon **lemon juice**

2 teaspoons **tomato paste**

Preparation
SERVES 4

1 Cook the noodles in plenty of boiling salted water according to
the package instructions, rinse in cold water and leave to drain.

2 Trim and wash the scallions and cut into rings. Peel the garlic.
Wash the beansprouts and leave to drain.

3 Heat a wok and add 1 tablespoon of the oil. Stir-fry the noodles
until crispy, remove and keep in a warm place. Add the rest of the
oil to the wok and stir-fry the shrimp. Add the crushed garlic and
fry with the shrimp.

4 After about 8 minutes take out the shrimp and keep warm. Now
stir-fry the scallions, adding the beansprouts and frying together
for 2 minutes.

5 Combine the cornstarch with the stock, and stir in the sambal
oelek, sugar, lemon juice and tomato purée. Pour into the wok and
bring to a boil, seasoning to taste with salt.

6 Divide the noodles between individual small bowls, arrange the
vegetables and shrimp on top and pour over the sauce.

**You can distinguish raw shrimp by their
greyish-blue color and shiny appearance.
They only become salmon pink in color
when immersed in boiling water.**

Squid
on a Bed of Vegetables

Do something challenging: Serving up this niftily prepared classic dish to company guarantees your guests will shower you with compliments

Ingredients

1 lb **squid**, tentacles removed

¾ cup **snow peas**

1 **yellow** and 1 **red pepper**

1 English **cucumber**

3 cloves **garlic**

2 **red chilies**

1 bunch Thai or ordinary **basil**

1 cup **beansprouts**

⅓ cup **peanut oil**

3 tablespoons **lime juice**

4 tablespoons **light soy sauce**

Preparation
SERVES 4

1 Wash the squid and pat dry. Cut open the body and score on the inside making a diamond grid pattern. Cut into 2-inch pieces.

2 Trim and wash the snow peas. Prepare and wash the peppers and cut into thin strips lengthways. Wash the cucumber, cut in half lengthways, take out the seeds and cut into thin strips. Peel the garlic, wash and seed the chilies and chop both finely.

3 Wash the basil, shake dry and pick off the leaves. Blanch the beansprouts for 2 minutes in boiling water and leave to drain.

4 Heat a wok and add 2 tablespoons of the oil. Stir-fry the pieces of squid. Add the chili and garlic and stir-fry for a further 5 minutes. Pour in the lime juice and soy sauce and stir well. Take out the pieces of squid and set aside in a warm place.

5 Heat up the remaining oil in the wok. Cook the snow peas and pepper strips. Add the strips of cucumber and beansprouts and continue to cook gently together for a short while. Add the pieces of squid to the mixture and stir in the basil leaves.

This dish tastes especially good when made with fresh squid. Alternatively you can use the same quantity of frozen squid rings.

Index

96

© Verlag Zabert Sandmann, Munich
Graphic design: Georg Feigl, Verena Fleischmann, Barbara Markwitz
Recipes: ZS-Team
Editing: Bärbel Schermer
Production: Karin Mayer, Peter Karg-Cordes
Lithography: inteca Media Service GmbH, Rosenheim
Printing & Binding: Officine Grafiche De Agostini, Novara
English translation: Translate-A-Book, Oxford, UK
American editor: Frances Cleary
Typesetting: Wakewing Typesetting Services, High Wycombe, UK

This edition published by Barnes & Noble, Inc.,
by arrangement with Zabert Sandmann.
2002 Barnes & Noble Books
M 10 9 8 7 6 5 4 3 2 1
Printed in Italy
ISBN 0-7607-2883-6

Visit us also on our Internet website at **www.zsverlag.de**

Photographic Credits

Cover photos: StockFood/Susie Eising (front); StockFood/S. & P. Eising (back cover left and center); StockFood/Susie Eising (back cover right)

Walter Cimbal: 17, 29, 43, 47, 71, 75, 76-77, 95; StockFood/Klaus Arras: 15; StockFood/Uwe Bender: 59; StockFood/Michael Brauner: 7/second from top left; StockFood/Jean Cazals: 10-11, 13, 26, 69; StockFood/Walter Cimbal: 2-3, 8; StockFood/Alack Chris: 49, 81, 89, 93; StockFood/James Duncan: 33, 57; StockFood/Eising: 7/top right; StockFood/Susie Eising: 4-5, 7/top left, 7/third from top left, 9, 18, 19, 22, 25, 27, 30-31, 36, 37, 44, 45, 51, 65, 66, 72, 73, 85, 91; StockFood/S. & P. Eising: 6/left, 7/bottom right, 23, 35, 39, 41, 52-53, 60, 61, 67, 79, 82, 83, 86, 87, 90; StockFood/Ulrike Köb: 21; StockFood/Kai Mewes: 55; StockFood/Maximilian Stock LTD: 6/right; StockFood/Viennaslide/Ellert: 7/4th from top left; StockFood/Jan-Peter Westermann: 63